I0624310

Making Plans
IN GOD'S WILL

9

The Single Sermon Series

Making Plans

IN GOD'S WILL

Joe Kappel

Publishing
Angel
Climbing

Making Plans in God's Will
Written by Joe Kappel

Transcribed and edited by Lisa Soland
Text copyright © 2024 Joe Kappel

Published in 2024 by:
Climbing Angel Publishing
PO Box 32381
Knoxville, Tennessee 37930
http://www.ClimbingAngel.com

First Edition: December 2024
Printed in the United States of America

Graphic Design: Climbing Angel Publishing

ISBN: 978-1-956218-40-4
Library of Congress Control Number: 2024925206

This book is dedicated to
Lauren,
the love of my life and partner in following
our Chief Shepherd.

Making Plans in God's Will

How many decisions do you think you make in a day? Let's consider this morning as an example. I bet you woke up because you decided to set an alarm on one of the many devices you probably have in your home to help you wake up. You chose the type of coffee or tea you wanted from the various options likely available in your pantry or on your shelf. You decided what to eat out of the several choices you had. You selected the clothing you would wear from the many items hanging in your closet. Even if it felt like you had limited options, you actually had many to choose from.

If it is Sunday, perhaps you made the choice to go to church. You probably drove there after selecting one of the vehicles you likely have in your garage or parked in your driveway. Reflecting on your morning, you realize you have already made at least six decisions—just a small fraction of the many more you will make throughout the day. We can draw one conclusion from this: you are a very wealthy individual.

Believers worldwide had fewer luxuries to choose from than we did this morning. Their options were much simpler. They didn't have alarms to wake them unless you consider oppressive heat and the cries of many children as alarms. They had very little to eat, so their only choice was to save what little food they had until lunchtime or dinner to sustain them for their one meal of the day. They didn't worry about picking out clothing because they already wore the same clothes they'd had on for several weeks. Additionally, they didn't have cars or even bicycles, so they walked several miles to get to their church. All of this was done out of a desire to worship God.

If you don't see yourself as very wealthy today, it may be time to change your perspective on what you use as a comparison. In this country, we have been incredibly blessed with the resources and opportunities God has given us and entrusted to us as stewards.

13 Come now, you who say, "Today or tomorrow we will go into such and such a town and spend a year there and trade and make a profit"— 14 yet you do not know what tomorrow will bring. What is your life? For you are a mist that appears for a little time and then vanishes. 15 Instead you ought to

say, "If the Lord wills, we will live and do this or that." 16 As it is, you boast in your arrogance. All such boasting is evil. 17 So whoever knows the right thing to do and fails to do it, for him it is sin.
(James 4:13-17)

The book of James was written to both kinds of people: the very wealthy and the poor. As James wrote, he reflected on the group of people God had assembled. In the opening verse, he referred to them as the "Twelve tribes in the Dispersion" (James 1:1). These individuals were scattered across various locations. They fled Jerusalem and escaped persecution while attempting to settle in different cities. James wrote to encourage them to remain steadfast in their faith and not be taken aback by the trials they were facing.

Relatively poor people and relatively wealthy people respond to challenges differently, and James attempts to address both groups simultaneously. He has called out the sins they are committing against one another. For instance, they have been arguing and trying to assert dominance over each other, a point mentioned several times in this letter. Additionally, they have been embracing worldly values, going so far as to reject the friendship of God Himself. They have also judged one another, as noted in Chapter 4, Verses 11 and 12, based on their social status rather than recognizing that there is only one judge over us all.

In James 4:13-17 and 5:1-6, the author shifts focus to a different category of sin, specifically addressing wealthy believers. In James 4:13-17, he seems to be speaking to individuals who believe, while in James 5:1-6, he directs his words towards unbelievers who are influenced by his letter.

1

MAKING PLANS

James admonished the wealthy believers of his time, and his message applies to us today, especially those of us enjoying freedom in the United States. We are fortunate to make thousands of decisions every morning and throughout the day. However, we have become complacent, believing we have complete mastery over our lives—ranging from the toothpaste we choose to the stocks we invest in—often without considering God's role in our choices. But as believers, we don't have to continue living this way. As described in James, Chapter 4, we have a God of all grace. This God accepts us as we are and addresses the sin of omission—the things we should do regarding God's Will and making plans. We can turn to the Word today, hoping God will change us.

I'm not saying that planning is wrong. We must plan for the future. In fact, it's essential and Biblically guided. However, you must do so with a humble submission to God today. The truth is, we can't do anything about a future we can't see or predict, but we can do something with the present we have right now.

We will study this text in relation to the concept of "will." The word "will" appears several times in James 4:13-17. So, first, I want to examine your "I will," and then we will *submit ourselves* to God's Will, then make plans and *do* God's Will.

Come now, you who say, "Today or tomorrow
we will go into such and such a town and
spend a year there and trade
and make a profit"—
(James 4:13)

Our text begins with James saying the words, "Come now." This expression shows his exasperation with how certain believers are living in this church. James is writing to them with the hope that they will recognize, through this needed rebuke, that what they are doing is wrong. Verse 17 says he's talking to people who know the right thing to do and are failing to do it. So, we see through a hypothetical situation that James is addressing some wealthy businessmen who are believers. Let's look at how they are responding to the trials they are facing. They're trying to say, *"Well, we have a lot of skills that we can put into practice, and we've been beaten down because of our Christianity and following the Messiah. But we are going to get back on top. We are going to make plans, and we're going to succeed!"*

James addresses these people by presenting this hypothetical situation. They are making plans, and although they say "we will," for the sake of our work in this book, I will use the phrase *"I will."* They say, *"I will go. I will spend a year there. I will trade and make a profit."* All of these statements are elements of planning or decision-making. And for the record, I want to say again that planning and decision-making are not bad. As a matter of fact, it's modeled throughout the Bible. Several times in the Book of Acts, Apostle Paul talks about how he is making plans. He talked about wanting to go to Spain. He spoke about how God ultimately directed him into a region of the world by closing down all of the other points on the compass. Finally, Paul ends up in the place where God wanted him all along, but Paul didn't know that until he started moving forward and making some plans. Making plans itself is not bad. These people are *doing things*, which is a wise place to start. Let's look at what they include in their decision-making process. I think this is important for us to see as well. Maybe some of you reading this are feeling paralyzed by what is happening in our culture and world today. Perhaps you have difficulty taking action. But we need to remember that "making plans" is good.

When we make a decision, we need a start date, a location, a goal, and an end date. What is it that you're trying to start? Where do you want to do it? What are the things that you're trying to accomplish? And when do you want to have it completed? All these things are helpful. James is not setting up a situation he wants to destroy by saying, *"Never take thought of these kinds of things."*

These are the elements that life insurance agents swim in. I read a story this week of a young guy who was talking to a life insurance salesman, trying to decide whether or not to buy a policy, and he ended up telling the agent, "I'm just really not sure right now." So, the agent looked at him and said, "Okay, I understand. If you think about it and change your mind, you can call me tomorrow if you wake up."

Regarding life insurance, investing, saving for retirement, and even saving for vacations or everyday needs, all these things are good and necessary and encouraged by godly principles. (Some reading this may need to get more serious about this type of planning and what you need to do with what God has given you.) But it's not a bad thing that the people in this text are planning. What's happening is that in their act of planning, they are taking God off of His throne by not acknowledging Him regarding things they are about to do. It's not wrong that they're making plans. It's not wrong that they're even making these particular plans. It's wrong that they're not thinking about God. This is a sin of *omission*. They know the right thing to do, but they're not doing it. So, James tells them to start evaluating life.

Yet you do not know what tomorrow will bring. What is your life? For you are a mist that appears for a little time and then vanishes.
(James 4:14)

The first thing James wants us to understand is that life is unpredictable. Let us remember Matthew 6:34:

"Therefore do not be anxious about tomorrow, for tomorrow will be anxious for itself. Sufficient for the day is its own trouble."

My family and I have been listening to a new song by Jess Ray lately. The chorus includes the phrase, "Don't waste today being scared of tomorrow." That is so true because tomorrow is not guaranteed. James encourages you to think about your limits and what you have no power over.

Each year, on 9/11, I try to watch some footage of the Twin Towers falling. Not because I have a macabre sense of humor or because I think that's fun. It's not fun. I do it so I can remember what happened in our country. I do it so I can think through what happened in a moment of time for the tragic demise of the people who were there that day. What's particularly troubling to me is watching the video footage of New Yorkers walking around on the streets of New York early on that morning, heading into the towers, having no idea that for many of them, their lives would end in a pile of rubble and dust. It hits me each time, and I wish I could speak through the TV back through the channels of time and warn them, but life doesn't work that way. We have this gift of "today" that the Lord has given us.

Jesus knew about this, and in His day, there was a tower that fell and killed a bunch of people, and He used that event as an opportunity to teach people the value of "today."

*3 No, I tell you; but unless you repent, you
will all likewise perish. 4 Or those eighteen
on whom the tower in Siloam fell and killed
them: do you think that they were worse
offenders than all the others who lived in
Jerusalem? 5 No, I tell you; but unless
you repent, you will all likewise perish."*
(Luke 13:3-5)

Knowing your limitations and accepting life's unpredictability can help you capitalize on "today" right now.

Some young people feel indestructible in their lives. If that is you, enjoy that feeling. It's a part of being young. But it does go away. Don't lose sight of the fact that you don't even have the guarantee of waking up tomorrow. But you do have "today." Have you made your life right with Christ? Before we go any further, that is the number one priority. That is the goal for you. That is the will of God for you—to seek Him. If you are not seeking Him, then today is the day that you must repent and turn to Jesus. If you have not done so, read these words carefully. Stop what you're doing, repent of your sins, and commit your life to Jesus Christ.

During my first year serving at West Park Baptist Church in Knoxville, Tennessee, I had an Adult Bible Fellowship director who would pray every time we met, "Heavenly Father, thank you for this unpromised day." He'd pray that same phrase every single time he prayed, and I began to find it formulaic and strange, but I took time to listen and consider the words. Now I realize how fitting that prayer truly is. We are not promised tomorrow, so when we wake up, we can thank God. *"This day wasn't promised to me, but you gave it to me as a gift. Thank you, God, for the gift of today!"*

We spend a lot of time either worrying about what we are trying to control or trying to control what could become a worry in the future. Instead, we need to capitalize on today. Life is too unpredictable. Make your plans and submit them to God with the full knowledge that you may not get there because of life's unpredictability. But honor God by preparing and communicating with Him regarding His priorities for your life.

> *Yet you do not know what tomorrow will bring. What is your life? For you are a mist that appears for a little time and then vanishes.*
> (James 4:14)

We have also learned that life is fleeting. James says you are a "mist that appears" briefly and then vanishes. He compares life to a mist or a vapor. I timed it at home. I sprayed a spray bottle, and the mist hung around about a second and a half. That's it. Then it was gone. I got out of the shower this morning, and the vapor from the steam made the mirror all foggy. I cleaned it off so I could see. And unless I were thinking about it now, I would have forgotten that mist forever. That vapor would be a long-lost idea. It is ancient history. We think about the family members we used to lean on and depend on for many things, but now they're gone. Maybe they've been gone for months or years, and we find it hard to think about them and remember them as we once did.

Our lives are the dash between our birth date and our death date. This is the description of a fleeting life. Beloved friends, it is the nature of our lives. When we think about life and these truths, we often feel uncomfortable. James presents these thoughts to increase that awkward feeling—not to destroy or depress us. But there are two ungodly responses to these things that we tend to adopt.

On the one hand, if this is true, someone may think that they've got to try to squeeze all the profit and pleasure out of life that they can right now. And in making this choice, many have veered off and completely missed eternal life with Jesus. On the other hand, some people think that life is so complex and fleeting that they're just going to retreat into their turtle shells and hide. That's wrong, too.

In Matthew 25:14-30, Jesus explains in a parable the story of a master who leaves his servants in charge of his wealth. He gave each of them a portion of what he thought they would need to steward. His desire for them was to increase that wealth. But the man who was given the least went and buried it, and when the master came back, he told the master, *"Well, I don't have any returns for you. I was afraid of you, and what you might do if I lost this, so I buried it for safekeeping."* The master was displeased with that servant and took what he had given to the man and gave it to the others. It is equally wrong to retreat and think about life's difficulties and not live in a way that takes risks to make plans, please God, and know Him better in this world. Both are wrong

We can feel the humbling of our lives, the squashing of the feeling that we don't have control over things like we once thought we did, the sicknesses that we've dealt with, the loved ones we've had to say goodbye to, the jobs we've lost, all the various things that squeeze us thin. But we realize over time, through God's grace and providence, that He is great and in control. The goal is not to be destroyed, waste our lives, run away, or retreat, but to instead submit ourselves to God.

2

SUBMITTING TO GOD'S WILL

In Verse 15, James offers the correct way of thinking.

Instead you ought to say, "If the Lord wills, we will live and do this or that."
(James 4:15)

Seeing life as unpredictable and fleeting in itself does not fix our problem. It's not even a Christian concept. The world knows these things, too. Philosophers abound in these thoughts—"life is unpredictable" and "life is fleeting." You see the same ideas in the book of Ecclesiastes: life is pointless unless you are pointed back to the One who holds your life in His hands.

The book of James is so rich with the theology of God. In James, Chapter 4, four things about God are worthy of our attention.

1. God is righteously jealous.

The first is this: God is righteously jealous to have complete devotion and worship from His beloved people, especially in light of our spiritual adultery. In James, Chapter 4:5 says, "He yearns jealously over the spirit that he has made to dwell in us"? God desires to have every single bit of our hearts. He desires you to submit to Him in every way and give up the many things you pursue for pleasure and purpose. There is no pleasure or purpose apart from the One who created us for Himself. God is righteously jealous for you.

2. He is the God of all grace.

Secondly, He is the God of all grace. When we think about the "jealous God," we imagine Him seeing us as spiritual adulteresses. We visualize Him seeking us out and catching us in our acts of unfaithfulness. We fear Him pulling out the Divine shotgun. But what does He actually do? "He gives *more* grace" (James 4:6). When you and I are at our worst and when we are at our best, we need God's grace. And that's what He provides.

In the book *The Discipline of Grace: God's Role and Our Role in the Pursuit of Holiness*, the author Jerry Bridges shared, "Our worst days are never so bad that you are beyond the reach of God's grace. And your best days are never so good that you are beyond the need of God's grace."

3. Draw near to Him.

Thirdly, we learn that God draws near to the one who draws near to Him even before, and maybe especially before, we clean up our act. Long before we denounce our sins, the command is to "Draw near to God" (James 4:8-9). Draw near to Him. That's the order of Christianity. Christianity does not demand you clean yourself up first and then come to God. The order is to come to God, and then, by His grace, He will help you by cleaning what you cannot.

4. God exalts us.

God exalts us or lifts us up when we humble ourselves before Him (James 4:10). This is our God! Why would you not structure every part of your life around this God? Why would you not center your entire life on Him?

So often, we try to control the outcomes of our lives, and we worry about what's going to happen, whether we are thinking about going for higher training somewhere, who we marry, where we'll live and work, planning out our family, investing, even trying to keep our families together. According to Verse 16, until we look to God the Father and see Him as absolutely sovereign and good, our attempts to control our lives and the outcomes we seek are nothing but boastful arrogance.

To combat this pride and arrogance in our hearts, James encourages us to say "if" instead of "I will." *If* the Lord wills. And this is not a formula. If you are making a tough decision and don't know if it will work out, you can't just throw a "If the Lord wills" in there. That is not the "special sauce" that makes your plan successful. This is an attitude that is more of the heart. It's good to say the words, but believing them and living by them in the heart is much better.

Sometimes, Apostle Paul said things like, "If the Lord wills, I'll do this," or "By the Lord's Will, I'll go here or there." Sometimes, he didn't say that at all, but the spirit and readiness were there to submit to God. It means knowing God and what pleases Him so we can do it. And leaving the Divine interruptions up to Him when He redirects our paths. This is good!

When I was in seminary, I told my roommate, "I will never go to China unless God gives me a wife." I had just sat through an appeal from a mission agency. They intended to get some of the guys who were still single with more mobility in their lives to go overseas, disciple the locals there, and raise up others who could do the same. It was exciting, but I did not want to be lonely. I did not want to be taken away from my support structure in the States. So I said those fateful words to my roommate, "I will never go to China..." and he just laughed at me. But if you know me, you know that I did go to China in 2005. I ended up there for several years. What changed my heart? I had a gap year between the time that I graduated from seminary and the time that I went overseas, and during that gap year, I lived alone, and God worked in my heart. I spent time in the Word and got to know Him better. I had to come to the point where I knew God and His intentions toward me. I had to come to a place where I didn't need all the answers regarding tomorrow, but instead, I grew confident that He would supply all my needs.

In the meantime, the girl who would become my wife was at West Park Baptist Church finishing her Mission Institute Training, preparing to go overseas to reach unreached tribal groups in Papa New Guinea. Praise the Lord, she was redirected to go through ABWE (Association of Baptists for World Evangelism) and ultimately ended up in Beijing, where I was pastoring a local church. I'm indebted to our pastor, Sam Polson of West Park, who gave her the nudge she needed!

I was excited to get to know Lauren. I was drawn to her initially and trying to sort out how, as a young guy pastoring a church, to have a relationship while under that unique microscope. But as I got to know her, I got to know her heart for those unreached people groups, and I knew that I didn't have a heart for unreached people groups in the same way she did. God had given me a heart for the local church where I was. As we talked about these things and as I perceived that I had the chance to get to know her better, we were hanging out once, and I asked her if she would be willing to let me be God's Will for her life. I asked her the best way I could, but I'm an awkward guy. I said, "I know you want to follow the Lord to reach tribal people, but we're getting closer, and I've got to know. Am I a monkey wrench thrown into God's Will for your life?" It was an awkward question from a nervous guy. But I will never forget how she looked at me. She smiled sweetly and said, "Not at all," and brothers and sisters, I knew then I was in.

While it seemed that God's Will for her during her teenage years was clear, and she wanted to go to those tribal regions of the world, we realized that God was redirecting our hearts to join together in His gracious will. Make no mistake, I chose to pursue Lauren, and she chose to let me, but God was the master planner. He rearranged our lives and worked His perfect Will.

That's how it works for us. We have to trust God and come to the point of completely submitting to His Will. Submitting to God's

Will means trusting and knowing Him. Then, we take the courageous steps to do what pleases Him, whatever that might mean for us. The Bible states it. And in your life, particular ways will seem to make sense the more you draw closer to Him.

3

DO GOD'S WILL

The third and final point is to make plans *and* do God's Will. This is taken from the last verse of our text, which says:

> *So whoever knows the right thing to do and fails to do it, for him it is sin.*
> (James 4:17)

This is not just about what we know intellectually in our heads. It's not just facts from the Bible. *It's a relationship of trust and obedience*. If you know what pleases God, which is having a relationship with Him, drawing near to Him, spending time with Him today, and receiving this gift of what you call "today," you can have great confidence that He will take you as far as He wants you to go.

Because that dash between your birth date and your death date is your life, and the only reason that dash exists is because God, in His will, has a purpose for you right now. Today.

Application #1:
Deal with Your Sin

First, I would like to encourage you to deal with your sin. It is sinful to live your life pretending that some parts are God's (maybe the Sunday stuff) but that the rest of the week is yours. Repent and turn to the Lord. James 4:10 says, "Humble yourselves before the Lord, and he will exalt you."

As you read these words, you may need to respond by recognizing that you've lived your life saying, *"Sunday belongs to God, but everything else belongs to me."* Perhaps it is time for you to see that way of living as sinful and wrong. I'm not saying you must pray, *"God, can I wake up today?"* And then go to your closet and say, *"God, what do you want me to wear?"* and wait until He tells you. And then go to the breakfast table and say, *"God, what do you want me to eat today?"* That is not the model of the New Testament guidance God provides us. The New Testament guides us to wake up thankful to God that we've woken up another day to serve and know Him. And to be a blessing to those people around you. Take the resources He's given you, and with an attitude of acceptance and reception of His ongoing work in your life, say, *"Lord, I'm launching out to do these things today. I'm excited about them. But if it's not what you want, I know you're a good God who will redirect me where you want me to go."* That kind of attitude is an attitude of submission, and if you're not there, you need to repent. Remember, your best days are not so good that you don't need God's grace. And your worst days are not so awful that you don't receive God's grace. He gives it to you. Come to Him. Draw near to Him.

Application #2:
Drop and Roll

The second application is to "Drop and Roll." This particular application refers to situations we all face, but not all of the time. So, this may affect some today, but it may not affect all of us. This point does not mean what to do if your clothes catch fire. However, "dropping and rolling" in the event of a fire is also a good tip.

I recently read a blog post by a woman who is still raising young kids and caring for aging parents. It's challenging because she's had to make some changes, and her personality is bent towards planning. She likes to-do lists. She likes to make detailed plans for each day of a vacation as well as detailed charts for every eventuality that her family might face. But when her life was stretched by what was required to care for her parents, she had to stop what she did so often, give up the lists she had made, and submit herself to the sovereignty of the Lord. In her words, she had to learn to *drop* what she was doing and *roll* with whatever God revealed. You may need to do that today: stop what you're doing and roll with whatever God brings to you.

There is a tradition in the Navy where the captain receives what are referred to as "sealed orders." A sealed envelope is delivered, and inside the envelope are instructions that contain a position on the map—longitude and latitude. The captain has to sail to that place, and when he gets there, he radios back to headquarters and asks for the next set of coordinates. What does this do? It teaches that the captain and his crew depend on the communications hierarchy and the chain of authority.

You and I may not respond well to authority, but we know that God, in His kindness, provides young believers with multiple evidences of His loving presence and provision. This may include quick answers to prayers and making things alive in your life. However, when we have been with the Lord for several years, it may feel like some things are not always so present and exciting. But God always gives just what we need to help us grow, as James has been discussing. He guides us to mature and walk with Him from one place to the next.

Application #3
A Personal Example

I hope the following recent and personal story provides a helpful example of a Christ follower working through an important decision-making process with full consideration of God's Will. Hoping to apply what I have learned while studying James, Chapter 4, I desire to seek out God's direction for my life as a lead pastor of a different church. As a result of executing the following actions, I believe the Lord is calling my family and me to do this.

Earlier this year, my pastor, Sam Polson, and I met and walked through what we see each of us doing in the next five years of ministry. I'll be 45 soon, and I thought, *"Man, 50 seems ancient."* (I'm kidding.) But I began to think, *"How can I invest this next season of my life? What's going to happen, Lord? What do you want me to do?"* I thought of myself here because I love my present church, and I want you to hear this clearly: there's nothing wrong. But my heart is to shepherd a flock, and there have been many times over the past few years that I've entertained the notion and looked at other opportunities with Pastor Sam. Each time he and I have prayed about this, a change just didn't seem right. So, he graciously had me remain on the team.

I have served at West Park for 11 years, and God has done so much in me. Pastor Sam has affirmed this desire of mine to shepherd a flock, and as far as he and I can see of the Lord's Will, this is the right move and the right time. We went to the elders, and they prayed over me in that meeting and affirmed that this seemed right as far as they could tell. I'm still waiting for somebody to come and tell me, "No, it's not right!" But that's just my nature. I want to make sure everything's done well. I also talked to the key staff members, and they agreed as well.

A good plan requires a start date and a place, and I have neither. But in the effort to step out in faith, I am using this example to show how plans may be great, but it is important to include God and His people in those plans.

All my fellow believers can help my family process this decision and pray for us. I have called for them to *not pull away* but to *lean in* and see what God will do for me and my family regarding my service to Him. I'm eager to see what that is even though I still need that start date, and I still need to get that place.

May God be pleased with my life. May I be sustained while waiting for my new assignment. And in your life, while you wait for your new plans to be fulfilled, friends, may you be sustained. "Waiting" in the Bible doesn't imply inactivity. Many good things are happening in all these communities, and as we continue to trust the Lord, let us step out in faith with confidence. And in such a time when the Lord redirects us, then the Lord will be kind to make clear to us His new plans for our lives.

Our Lord Jesus went through significant upsets during His earthly life. Some plans did not work out according to what those around Him thought they should. Yet, Jesus said in the garden, "Father, if you are willing, remove this cup from me. Nevertheless, not my will, but yours, be done" (Luke 22:42). He said, "Not my will, but yours, be done." Our Lord Jesus understood this matter of submission to God's Will. All around Him were people *not* submitting to God's Will—the religious leaders, the pagans in the Jewish community, the Gentiles, and even His disciples in many ways. Jesus went into the garden and sweated great drops of blood, and He cried out to the Father, "If it is Your will, let this cup pass from Me." What was the cup? It was the cup of His

Divine wrath for your sin and mine. Jesus took it and drank it all so that when you and I come together to examine His Word or to worship Him, we can be reminded of two things: the cup that we deserved, Jesus drank. And the cup we don't deserve, we get to participate in remembering Jesus' atoning sacrifice until His return.

PRAYER

Oh Lord, we are in desperate need of your grace. In the garden, you cried out, "Father, let this cup pass from me, and yet, not what I will but what you will." Please help us to say those words when we struggle with our own desires. Grant us the grace to repent and turn to you, fully expecting your forgiveness and grace. Guide us in our daily lives, and help us to execute your will. Our lives are in your hands. We ask for clarity in your plans for us, knowing you open doors no one can shut.

Lord, thank you for bringing us into the kingdom for such a time as this. Each day, we give ourselves to you afresh and anew. We trust in you, the one who can do exceedingly and abundantly above all that we ask or think according to your power that is at work in us. May there be glory in the church and through Christ Jesus forever. Amen.

ABOUT
CLIMBING ANGEL PUBLISHING

Climbing Angel Publishing shares stories of hope and encouragement, aids in the gathering together of community, and supports the process of betterment. The following books are available at your leading online bookstores.

ADULT BOOKS: (Romans 8:28-30)

In His Image by Sam Polson
(English, Romanian, Mandarin, & Spanish)
By Faith by Sam Polson (English & Romanian)
My Birthday Gift to Jesus by Lisa Soland
Without Ceasing by Dr. Dennis Davidson
SonLight: Daily Light from the Pages of God's Word
by Sam Polson
Corona Victus: Conquering the Virus of Fear
by Sam Polson (English & Romanian)
*Art Bushing: His Diary, Letters, & Photographs of
WWII* by Art Bushing
*Art & Dotty: His Diary, Their Letters & Photographs of
WWII* by Art Bushing
Trimisul by Stan Johnson (Romanian)
Life Changing Prayer by Sam Polson
The Climbing Angel Christmas Treasury,
variety of authors
J. Calvin Coolidge: Letters from the Korean War
by J. Calvin Coolidge
*Stories from Kingman, AZ: The Heart of Historic Route
66* by Loren B. Wilson
*Pathways: Ancient Paths from the Pages of the Old
Testament* by Sam Polson
Fear Not by Sam Polson

THE SINGLE SERMON SERIES: (1 Pet. 3:15)

Jesus is Alive! by Mike Sager
My Mother's Bible by Sam Polson
The Lost Boys by Jake Bishop
Melchizedek: A Shadow of Christ by Jerry Scheumann
A Servant of Christ by James Alan Lynch
Dreaming God's Dream by Dr. Al Cage
Resisting Sin by Colin Hughes
A Call to Christians by Chris Reed
Making Plans in God's Will by Joe Kappel

CHILDREN'S BOOKS: (Philippians 4:8)

The Christmas Tree Angel by Lisa Soland
The Unmade Moose by Lisa Soland
Thump by Lisa Soland
Somebunny To Love by Lisa Soland
(English & Mandarin)
The Truth About God's Rainbow by Lisa Soland
God's Promises by Lisa Soland
The Boy & The Bagel Necklace by Lisa Soland
God's Hands and Feet by Lisa Soland
I Like To Be Quiet by Joni Caldwell
Wheels Off! by Karlie Saumier
Ella's Trip of a Lifetime by Melanie Ewbank
Because You Are Mine by Gayle Childress Greene
Jeremy Plays the Blues by Amy Oden Simpson
Bad Hair Day by Jasmyne Simpkins
I Like To Read by Joni Caldwell
Trunks Up! by Karlie Saumier
Perusha's Paradise by Bette Reed Smith
Ruby and the Treasure Within
by Tonya Celeste Hobbs
Abby, the Wonder Dog & her Warrior Princess
by Melanie Ewbank
The Christmas Coat by Lisa Soland
Danger Around the Bend by Karlie Saumier